Open to the Spirit

St Ignatius and John Wimber in Dialogue

Robin Stockitt

Curate, St Andrew's and All Saints,
Billing, Northants

GROVE BOOKS LIMITED
RIDLEY HALL RD CAMBRIDGE CB3 9HU

Contents

Acknowledgement

My thanks go to Revd Andy Hawes of Edenham Regional House, Lincolnshire
for his support and encouragement over the years.

The Cover Illustration   consists of the logos of the Jesuits and the Vineyard movement

First Impression November 2000
ISSN 0262-799X
ISBN 1 85174 448 7

1
The Gift of Dissatisfaction

For years I have been troubled with feelings of dissatisfaction. My spiritual journey has taken me through the varied landscapes of the Christian world and at every stage I have found something that nourishes and teaches. And yet I have also felt that there must, surely, be more to experience of God than each particular approach to prayer and discipleship offers. I have been dissatisfied and at times felt guilty about that. Now I wonder whether that sense of dissatisfaction is actually a prompting of the Holy Spirit. My search has been for a spirituality that can contain the ambiguities and uncertainties of life whilst simultaneously enabling me to follow Christ with courage and freedom. It is my conviction that by drawing upon the rich resources of different traditions our own growth can be best served.

For more than a decade I have inhabited two very different worlds—the Ignatian and the Vineyard. Both worlds emphasize the work of the Holy Spirit and in that sense they are both truly charismatic. Yet they come from very different ends of the spectrum of church traditions and do not appear to have met or understood one another. The major difficulty, I suspect, is with language. If a way of speaking is alien to us it simply requires too much effort and patience to understand what is being said. Who within the Vineyard movement could understand Ignatius when he writes about the 'First Principle and Foundation' or the 'three rules for making a sound election.' What *does* this mean? Likewise for those immersed in Ignatian spirituality, the Vineyard emphases on 'anointing,' on 'words and pictures' or 'demonization' are confusing if not thoroughly disturbing. Those who are familiar with the language that is used to convey concepts have no problems. When that language is employed in 'alien' territory suspicions and barriers are erected.

Can we bring these two worlds together? Why should we bother? Surely these two approaches to spirituality are so divergent that they never actually meet each other, they have no common threads, they come from different traditions within the Christian church. Perhaps it is better to leave them where they are.

However, both Ignatian and Vineyard spirituality remain powerful influences on large sections of the Christian church. Although Ignatius wrote his *Exercises* in the early part of the sixteenth century they are still widely used today. They have enjoyed considerable resurgence in Britain, principally under the influence of Gerard Hughes, a Jesuit who lived and worked for a time at St Beuno's in North Wales, and Philip Sheldrake who edited the Ignatian magazine *The Way* for many years. Their desire (and that of others) to see the *Exercises* made more widely available outside Roman Catholic religious life has contributed signficantly to their growing popularity in all parts of the Christian church.

The Vineyard movement similarly exerts a significant influence in charismatic circles. Founded in the late 1970s in California largely through the leadership of John Wimber, there are now Vineyard churches all over the world. In the 1980s John Wimber made frequent visits to the United Kingdom to conduct conferences and his considerable appeal to the British culture lay, to a large extent, in his relaxed undemonstrative style, combined with a disarming honesty about personal weakness and failure.

During these visits he forged relationships with a number of ministers in the Church of England. Amongst these were Revd David Watson from York, Canon Robert Warren from Sheffield and Bishop David Pytches in Chorleywood. It was David Pytches who was instrumental in establishing an event entitled 'New Wine' which embodies the values and principles of the Vineyard movement and attracts many thousands of people. This annual conference has been instrumental in bringing together certain elements of the house church movement with sections of the Anglican church.

So why should St Ignatius talk to John Wimber? Or more pertinently, what is there to gain for their offspring if they dialogue? The danger for any 'movement' within the Christian church is for its proponents to remain in a self-contained world, where all the complexities and difficulties of life are understood and interpreted through one filter. When just a single lens is used to understand and interpret our place within God's world then it is possible to limit the way God engages with us. Our horizons become rather too clearly defined, our checks and balances may become a little skewed and what began as an initiative from God becomes formalized, crystallized, bottled and preserved. The freshness and spontaneity of the Holy Spirit can be reduced to a formula for 'success.' So, I believe that there is much to be gained from being open to other approaches to spiritual growth. After all, as Gerard Hughes puts it, God is a God of surprises.[1]

1   Gerard Hughes, *God of Surprises* (London: DLT, 1987).

2
Origins

Before we examine in detail the particular emphases of these two approaches it is important to understand their origins.

Ignatius

Born in 1491 in the Basque town of Azpeitia, Ignatius came from a noble family. In his early life he worked as the page of the royal treasurer and accompanied his master to the royal court.[2] He later became a soldier and was involved in the siege of Pamplona by the French in 1521. It was here that his life changed dramatically when he was injured by a cannonball in his leg. The fracture was set and reset resulting in a convalescence which lasted nearly 10 months. During this period his encounters with God were particularly formative. He noticed that when he dreamt of doing heroic deeds on the battlefield, the experience left him feeling drained and exhausted. By contrast when he imagined himself performing great adventures for the sake of Christ he felt invigorated and refreshed. It was by paying attention to the 'movements within his soul' that he was persuaded to completely alter the course of his career. His dissatisfaction with the way he had been living was highlighted by the allure of following Christ. It was as if he was being divinely courted. This attentiveness to God's actions within him became a key feature of his spiritual development. From that time onwards he vowed that he would be a soldier for Christ. He exchanged his clothes for those of a poor man, he went on a pilgrimage to Jerusalem, he studied avidly, both in Paris and in Rome and had a number of significant spiritual experiences which shaped his values and changed the course of his life. One of these occurred in Manresa in 1522 where he remained for several months. During this time he had a visionary experience in a cave on the banks of the river Cardoner. From that point onwards,

> He saw Jesus as the gentle king and lord who came to fulfil the spread of the kingdom of God which had dawned. Ignatius sensed his vocation to become a worker with and for Christ.[3]

Over the next few years he began to write down the insights he gained from such experiences in his book, *The Spiritual Exercises.*

The *Spiritual Exercises* take the participant on a course of prayer—and yet they are far more than that. They are about spiritual formation, about conversion of the heart and soul, and they are about becoming a companion of Christ in his life and in his death. They are divided into four 'weeks' or stages and are based around

---

2   Karl Rahner and Paul Imhof, *Ignatius of Loyola* (London: Collins, 1978) p 49.
3   *Ibid*, p 52.

meditations on the life of Christ. In each 'week' there is a 'theme' which provides a focus. In week one, for example, the emphasis is on asking for the grace to be given a fresh understanding of God and of our place in his creation. The purpose of the exercises is to enable people to make a choice—an election—to follow Christ wherever that may lead. In order to make 'an election' various suggestions and guides are given so that the person who is undertaking the exercises learns to discern and respond to the ongoing work of the Holy Spirit. These include, for example, using the five senses to enter imaginatively into the text of Scripture, paying close attention to the pattern of one's emotional life, learning to respect the boundaries and limits of one's own discernment and using a guide or mentor as a sounding board. Ignatius envisaged that anyone, both clerical and lay, could use his exercises, that each person should proceed at their own speed as God directed them and that the spiritual guide should use a light touch in helping others to discover God.

John Wimber

John Wimber's experiences of God's work within him similarly proved to be highly formative. A pastor of a Quaker congregation in California in the 1970s, he had begun to feel a certain level of frustration and disappointment not only with his own ministry but with many aspects of the established churches. He left local church ministry for a while and lectured in a nearby seminary. When a small group of Christians began meeting in a home in Anaheim they asked Wimber to be their pastor. Many of these people had been wounded and exhausted through many years of involvement in church life. What drew them together was a common desire to feel and experience the touch of the Holy Spirit in their lives. They would spend long periods of time singing worship songs and longing for 'intimacy' with Christ. Teaching from the Scriptures by Wimber was followed by prayer for 'healing' through the laying on of hands. In the simplicity, almost naïvete, of those early days extraordinary manifestations of God were seen. People would regularly weep, laugh, fall over, speak in tongues and experience powerful encounters with the Holy Spirit. It was as if this group of Christians had accidentally stumbled across the same kind of experiences as are recorded in the book of Acts.

Needless to say this proved to be enormously appealing. The little house church soon outgrew its premises, became a church with a membership of several thousand and spawned similar congregations across the United States. Within a few years Wimber and his team had visited Britain and were 'doing the stuff' (as Wimber used to put it) in front of huge conferences. His teaching that we are called only to 'do what the Father is doing' (John 5.19) with his encouragement that any Christian has access to all the gifts of the Spirit, acted as a catalyst for many Christians for whom following Christ had become arid and filled with duty. Wimber represented a childlike simplicity combined with natural, Spirit-given joy. With Wimber the concept of 'the baptism in the Spirit,' which had been so divisive in the 1960s, was not an issue. There was no personality cult and 'power' did not reside solely with the leadership. This was the Holy Spirit offered and available to all. Ordinary Christians felt empowered and valued. Here was an approach to God that allowed them to lay on hands and expect God to work. Here was someone who encouraged them to seek all the gifts that God had to offer. Here at last was a taste of heaven on earth, God breaking into our humdrum lives in astonishing displays of power. It is hardly surprising that Wimber's influence has been profound.

Points of Contact

A superficial exploration of these two approaches may suggest that there are very few points of contact. Vineyard conferences can be noisy, untidy and attended by thousands. Ignatian retreats are orderly, silent and enjoyed by just a few individuals. Wimber's emphasis on rediscovering the immediacy of the Holy Spirit and allowing God space to work appears to have little in common with the work of Ignatius and his formalized set of exercises written centuries ago. Indeed, Ignatius barely mentions the Holy Spirit at all except for a few isolated references to the Trinity.[4]

Yet for both men their theology began with and was given impetus by their experiences of God. The key to understanding the life and influence of Ignatius is his recurring phrase which in Spanish is '*de arriba*,' meaning 'from above.'[5] It was because he had experienced a profound movement of God within him that he was able to develop his later insights. For Ignatius true understanding began with God's initiative in his life. His task was to respond to that initiative, to make sense of it and to use it to guide his affections and his will. His whole theology was 'from above.' David Lonsdale writes:

> It is clear from Ignatius' autobiography that experience was the main catalyst of change in his life. For Ignatius, growth was not a matter of first having a theory and then trying to bring his practice into line with his theory…rather he noted the main features of his own experience and reflecting on them saw in them signs of God's presence and action.[6]

With such a starting point Ignatius developed an approach to prayer that was accessible for all people. It was not something that became the exclusive domain of religious communities. Ordinary working people were encouraged to embark on the *Exercises* and to discover God for themselves. Ignatius encouraged people to seek a direct encounter with God for themselves. He was doing for lay people what Wimber did centuries later—giving people hope.

---

4   The lack of direct references to the Holy Spirit in the work of Ignatius is not the result of an ill-formed theology of the Spirit. Ignatius was living at a time of great ecclesiastical sensitivity where mention of the Spirit was likely to arouse very strong antagonistic reactions. His relative 'silence' on the subject was a sign of his astuteness rather than his ignorance.
5   Hugo Rahner, *Ignatius the Theologian* (Geoffrey Chapman, 1990) p 3.
6   David Lonsdale SJ, *Eyes to See, Ears to Hear* (London: DLT, 2000) p 56.

Allowing God to take the initiative was manifestly true for Wimber. For many years he had been wary of displays of emotion or strange manifestations of the Spirit, particularly speaking in tongues. It was only when he experienced an unusual outpouring of the Holy Spirit one Sunday during a church service in 1979 that he went back to the Scriptures and church history to re-evaluate his theology. The result of this process was what Wimber termed a 'paradigm shift.' By this he meant a thorough reshaping of his whole theological perspective. It was for Wimber a pivotal moment when he not only saw what was possible under the power of the Spirit, but realized what 'the coming of the kingdom' meant for the present day. This is how Wimber himself expresses it:

> God uses our experiences to show us more fully what he teaches in Scripture, many times toppling or altering elements of our theology and world views. This is what he accomplished with the disciples through their experience of his crucifixion and resurrection.[7]

The key point for both men was that in sensing the presence of God in their own lives they subsequently sought to develop a theological framework within which they could contain and interpret their experiences. It was not that their rationality had become redundant but rather it had become the servant of their experience. For both men the starting point of their theology—experience—influenced everything that followed. The pressing need was to make sense of God's overtures. If intimacy with Christ was discovered by responding to the divine initiative then it followed that the one overriding concern was to learn to discern what God was doing and to cooperate with him in that process.

---

7   John Wimber, *Power Evangelism* (Hodder and Stoughton, 1985) p 94.

3
Discernment—The Heart of It All

How did these men approach the thorny question of discovering the will of God? For Ignatius, God's will was not understood to be a huge blueprint upon which the future had already been mapped out in detail with our task being merely to find the corner that was relevant to our situation. Rather, God's will was conceived in a far more dynamic way, an interweaving of our free responses and choices with God's purposes. There would always be a creative tension where God was continually calling, inviting a response of love from us. The desire to sense God's will was paramount for Ignatius and he rarely concluded any of his letters without expressing the wish that his readers would 'feel the will of God in order that they may fulfil it perfectly.'[8] It was because of the centrality of this in his thinking that Ignatius devoted much of his energies to developing guidelines for the 'discernment of spirits.'

Indifference and Attentiveness
    The first of these was that discernment occurred within the context of prayer and that as we approach a time of prayer we need to be in a state of 'indifference.' By this he was referring to a disposition of openness. This is how Ignatius puts it:

> It is necessary to keep as aim the end for which I am created, which is to praise God our Lord and save my soul, and, this supposed, to find myself indifferent, without any inordinate propensity; so that I be not more inclined or disposed to take the thing proposed than to leave it, nor more to leave it nor more to take it, but find myself as in the middle of a balance, to follow what I feel to be more for the glory and praise of God our Lord and the salvation of my soul.[9]

The reason for this injunction is not hard to find. Ignatius was aware of the subtle deceptions of the human psyche, how easy it is to persuade oneself that one has discovered the will of God when in reality the outcome had already been decided in secret beforehand. Not only was it possible for us to deceive ourselves, Ignatius believed, but he was also aware of a spiritual adversary, Satan, who was intent upon destruction and confusion. Thus Ignatius urged his students to approach God in a state of 'indifference,' a condition which describes contentment with the work of God in our lives, whatever that may be. Ignatius likened indifference to a balanced set of weighing scales, believing that by being in a state of equilibrium

---

8   Hugo Rahner, *Ignatius*, p 147.
9   Paragraph 179 taken from *The Spiritual Exercises of St Ignatius*, translated by David Fleming, SJ (St Louis: Institute of Jesuit Sources, 1978) p 108.

we are more likely to be truly open to whatever God is saying to us.

The second principle of Ignatian discernment concerns paying close attention to the affective movements within the soul. These are the kind of involuntary feelings and moods that arise often, but not solely, as a result of meditating upon the Scriptures. In the course of everyday life each of us faces a bewildering array of experiences, desires, impulses, revulsions and attractions. Many of these operate on a superficial level. Ignatius was concerned with the more profound affective moments, those critical times when decisions need to be made which have an effect on the direction of our lives even though we may not understand the origin of these feelings or what they mean.

Discernment and Direction

In the 'discernment of spirits' Ignatius was concerned with discovering a spiritual interpretation of what was happening. In what direction do these emotions draw us? Towards God or away from him?

Ignatius noticed that some emotions pull us towards God and help us to be 'less centred upon ourselves and more open to others. We might feel, for example, a sense of gratitude to God that leads to a deeper faith, trust and love or a joyful awareness and appreciation of the presence and action and gifts of God in people.'[10] Alternatively we may feel a keen sense of sorrow over our own infidelities in following Christ, even to the point of tears. It is at times like this when prayer is easy, when repentance is offered and our relationship with God is characterized by joy that Ignatius terms 'times of consolation.' These occasions are pure gifts of God's grace. They are not rewards for good behaviour, they are not earned, they are simply given.

By contrast, 'times of desolation' have the opposite effect. They draw us away from God. They cause us to be more closed in and unconcerned about God or about other people. There may be a depressing darkness, an emptiness, restlessness or anxiety. The crucial issue however in evaluating our feelings in discernment is not so much where the feelings come from, nor indeed what those emotions are, but the direction in which the feelings are leading. The question is whether our lives are moving towards or away from God. It is possible, argued Ignatius, to experience feelings of consolation yet be to be moving away from the heart of God. He recognized this as false consolation. Equally, experiences of desolation may occur during times of serious searching for the will of God. For Ignatius the overriding concern was that our lives are to be lived for the greater glory of God. At times of desolation this sense of purpose can disappear and be replaced by a preoccupation with one's own private agenda. Ignatius recognized the inevitability of having to experience such times. His advice was to recognize that they will, in time, pass. No major decisions should be made when one is experiencing a period of desolation.

---

10   David Lonsdale SJ, *Eyes to See*, p 98.

'What the Father is Doing'

For Wimber the discernment of the heart of God was similarly critical. Wimber had had many years experience of working hard in evangelism, in setting up programmes of Christian education and discipleship and in many other aspects of church life. His 'paradigm shift' caused him to question not only the effectiveness of these strategies but also their validity in the light of his motto text that we are called to 'do only what the Father is doing.' This was the model of ministry he observed in the life of Jesus and thus became his guiding principle. But how do we know 'what the Father is doing'?

In his attempt to answer this question Wimber was heavily influenced by the work of George Ladd, whose book *The Theology of the New Testament* gave Wimber a fresh understanding of the 'kingdom of God.'[11] According to Ladd this present age, from creation to the final judgment, is characterized by human weakness, mortality, evil, sin and death. The kingdom of God is currently breaking into this age, with the church as its instrument. Therefore the task of Christians is to enlist in this spiritual warfare and be used by God to bring the kingdom into being. And to do this we are given power and authority by Christ to fulfil his commission. Wimber writes:

The works of the kingdom are performed through us, thus our purpose is to witness about what God has done, is doing and will do. Like Jesus we have come to do the will of the Father…we must learn to hear and believe Jesus' commands if we expect to do signs and miracles.[12]

Wimber's approach thus places a strong emphasis on listening to God and waiting to hear what God is saying. His emphasis on the 'kingdom of God' provided a set of expectations concerning what was possible within this discernment process. Thus Wimber fully expected to receive words of knowledge, pictures, dreams, visions, tongues, impressions and strong feelings about the right course of action to take. Wimber placed great store on such affective responses to God. Sometimes specific words would 'appear' which provided the key to unlock a situation. At other times a picture would be given which, when interpreted correctly, discerned the will of God for an individual or a particular situation. Whenever such gifts were given it was simply the task of the Christian to cooperate with what God had revealed about himself. One should expect signs and wonders to follow.

Wimber recounts this story from his own experience to illustrate his point. He was travelling on a plane and had just settled into his seat when he noticed a man sitting opposite him.

In the split second my eyes happened to be cast in his direction, I saw something that startled me. Written across the man's face in very clear and distinct

11   George Eldon Ladd, *A Theology of the New Testament* (Guildford: Lutterworth Press, 1974).
12   *Power Evangelism,* p 26.

letters I thought I saw the word 'adultery'…as the man spoke a woman's name came into my mind.[13]

Wimber then goes on to explain how this 'word' from God, after some conversation had taken place between the two of them, unlocked that man's heart and he came to the point of repentance and faith in Christ.

Wimber's final words in his book *Power Evangelism* sum up his whole approach:

God gives impressions, and we act on them. If he does not speak to us, then we wait.[14]

Although Wimber's somewhat unusual story may sound strange to us, he would argue that the account of the Ethiopian coming to faith in Acts 8 is in the same category. At the heart of Wimber's approach is the desire to hear the voice of God. This does not seem very far away from the discernment process outlined by Ignatius. Both men start with waiting to sense the heart and mind of God. Only when this has been perceived do we make a move. The crucial issue here is how one 'waits' upon God. How is the voice of God heard?

Using the Senses

What is most striking in this regard is the use that is made of the senses to facilitate discernment. Vineyard practice is filled with examples of images that are 'seen' in the imagination, words that are 'heard' and bodily sensations. Great significance is attached to these manifestations as they are viewed as ways in which God speaks today. To support this claim reference is made to the gospels and the book of Acts which are filled with unusual and strange occurrences. Wimber's whole approach to discernment involved not simply the rational, intellectual study of Scripture which forms a major foundation of the Vineyard movement, but also an openness to the use of the imagination and sensory experiences. Wimber's rationale was that we must expect that God can and indeed does engage with humankind in just the same way as he did in the days of the early church. To deny that this is possible is to place limits on the activity of the Holy Spirit and thereby to emasculate the church. One of Wimber's most memorable phrases was 'God wants his church back,' and by this he was referring to a group of people who were prepared to let God use them however he chose. If this meant that God would speak through dreams, visions, voices and pictures then these should be welcomed.

The use of the imagination and the five senses similarly forms a central part of Ignatian spirituality. However, the difference here lies in the context in which imagination is used. For Ignatius this should be whilst meditating on the Scrip-

---

13   *Power Evangelism*, p 44.
14   *Power Evangelism*, p 150.

tures themselves, and more specifically whilst using the gospel accounts of the life of Christ. To facilitate this Ignatius suggested that at times it is useful to make an 'application of the senses.' By this he meant that in contemplating on a text of Scripture the passage is enriched and comes alive when all five senses are deployed. He writes:

The first point is to see the persons (in the biblical story) with the sight of the imagination, meditating and contemplating in particular the details about them...the second to hear with the hearing what they may be talking about, the third to smell and taste, the fourth to touch the places where the persons put their feet and sit...[15]

By using such a creative approach to Scripture reading and prayer Ignatius was concerned to draw out every ounce of God's grace from each text. Scripture must touch not just the mind but the heart as well. This synthesis of mind and heart is what takes place in the 'application of the senses.' There can be a gap between the way we form prayer in our heads and the way we experience prayer in our hearts. Ignatius use of the senses was designed to address this particular issue.

In Vineyard spirituality, imaging the work of Jesus today is not so firmly tied to the Scripture text. An example of this can be seen in one of the distinctive features of Vineyard practice over the past couple of decades—that of 'prayer ministry.' Prayer ministry is a common feature of a normal Vineyard service and is employed to invoke the work of the Spirit in a specific way to help an individual. Mary Pytches, writing from her experience in an Anglican setting, describes a typical prayer ministry encounter:

One young man arranged an interview explaining that he suffered from crippling anxiety. During the time together I became aware of a recurring phrase, 'I must never make a mistake.' Realizing the cause of the belief was buried in his unconscious, I suggested we pray and ask God to show us where it came from. I prayed and waited. After a short while the man began to cry as if he were again a small boy. Eventually he told me that God had taken him back to his school where he was sent at the tender age of five. In this school, rigid discipline had been maintained and the boys were beaten for any small mistake. Fear had taken root in the little boy's heart and whenever he needed to make a decision today the old irrational belief came into play.[16]

To those unfamiliar with the practice this may seem bizarre and intrusive, to those who have benefited from it, it is often found to be a major stepping stone in the process of growth and maturity. The activity normally involves one or two people praying for a third person. If, during the time of prayer, the Holy Spirit reveals

15 *Spiritual Exercises*, paragraphs 122 to 125.
16 Mary Pytches, *Set My People Free* (Hodder and Stoughton, 1987) pp 34–35.

an issue or an event to an individual that has become a stumbling block, then at that point Jesus is invited to enter and bring healing. The incident may be recent or from many years ago, but time is immaterial once Jesus enters the picture. The task of those praying for healing is simply to ask the Holy Spirit to work, and to cooperate with whatever happens next.

Many people have found this type of prayer to be enormously beneficial. But what is interesting is that it is not very far away from one of the spiritual exercises suggested by Ignatius. Ignatius offered a structure for prayer. It was not prescriptive but simply provided the framework within which prayer could take place. One of the elements he suggested was to engage in a 'colloquy.' By this he meant a conversation, a dialogue between Christ and the individual. He writes:

> Imagining Christ our Lord present and placed on the cross, let me make a colloquy, how from Creator he is come to making himself man, and from life eternal is come to temporal death and to die for my sins. Likewise looking at myself what I have done for Christ what I am doing for Christ what I ought to do for Christ…the colloquy is made as one friend speaks to another.[17]

This exercise is designed to strike at the heart of our affections and desires. To gaze into the eyes of Christ dying on the cross and at that place to enter into conversation is indeed a life-changing activity. This is very similar to allowing Christ to be present in the context of prayer ministry. In both types of prayer it is the direct relationship with Christ, the dialogue, the meeting, that produces such a powerful and potentially healing encounter.

What is happening here in the use of the imagination and the senses for both Ignatian and Vineyard theology is a 'making present' of the past. It is similar to the act of 'remembering' which would have been well known to the Jewish mind. Biblical 'remembering'[18] is far more than simply recalling past events, it is reliving those events by bringing them into the present moment. Jewish communities remember the Passover because in a very real sense they were there at that momentous shaping of the nation of Israel. Christians 'remember' the death of Christ in the act of celebrating communion, they become present at the Last Supper, at the foot of the cross. It is by re-entering the past in this way that the past becomes alive and retains its power to transform the present. The Ignatian application of the senses and use of the colloquy and the Vineyard use of 'prayer ministry' both employ variant forms of 'remembering.' For Ignatius it is a question of making oneself present in the biblical text and encountering Christ there. By indwelling the biblical story it becomes our own.[19] In Vineyard spirituality the emphasis is on 'remembering' one's own past and inviting Christ to meet with us at pivotal moments. Both approaches acknowledge that God uses the power of remembering to further his healing presence.

17 *Spiritual Exercises*, paragraph 53.
18 *anamnesis* in the Greek. See Luke 22.19, 1 Cor 11.24, 25.
19 J R Middleton and B J Walsh, *Truth is Stranger Than It Used To Be* (London: SPCK, 1995).

4
Checks and Balances to Discernment

Discernment is at the heart of both forms of spirituality, but it is surely an activity which is fraught with danger. Ignatius was concerned to avoid excesses. He therefore urged those using his exercises to submit themselves firstly to the authority of the church. He insisted that there needs to be a resonance with the corporate life of the church, the private discernment of the individual and a way of life that is compatible with a profession of faith. Ignatius also insisted that all discernment must be conducted within the context of contemplating the life of Christ as revealed in the gospels. If the whole purpose of discernment was to enable greater obedience to Christ and conformity to his character, then meditation on his life was of paramount importance. This is expressed well by Rahner:

> During the exercises the exercitant should not direct his attention simply to the movements of the spirits going on within him, but rather to the love of God which both proceeds and accompanies all movements of the soul and he will do this by continuing to contemplate the mysteries of the life of Christ.[20]

If the fruit of the discernment process did not result in a greater awareness of Christ's claims or a greater conformity of character then clearly something had gone awry and needed correction.

Ignatius was keen to point out that it was facile to draw too sharp a distinction between 'consolation' and 'desolation,' with the former being unfailingly beneficial and the latter always being destructive. He was aware that times of desolation can be very instructive and be times of growth. The feelings of desolation were not in themselves destructive. They only become so when we acted upon those feelings or made choices under the influence of them. Ignatius suggested that we should avoid making important decisions during these times because they could lead us in the wrong direction altogether. Times of desolation, according to Ignatius, could be occasions when God:

> …gives us true acquaintance and knowledge, that we may interiorly feel that it is not ours to get or keep great devotion, intense love or tears or any other great spiritual consolation but that all is the gift and grace of God.[21]

Not only are we to draw benefit from times of desolation, we need to be aware that times of consolation can be false. Ignatius was conscious of the subtlety of the human psyche, how easy it is to deceive oneself or be deceived. So how are we to

---

20   Hugo Rahner, *Ignatius the Theologian*, p 146.
21   *Spiritual Exercises*, paragraph 322.

distinguish between true consolation and its counterfeit? Ignatius offers several pointers. The first is to recognize the deceitful wiles of the devil who constantly acts as an adversary to those who want to follow Christ. The second is to trace back the steps that have been taken which produced a harmful or destructive result, to notice at which point things began to go wrong, and the third is to seek the advice of someone else. Listen to the words of Ignatius again:

> In the same way when the enemy of our human nature tempts a just soul with his wiles and seductions, he earnestly desires that they be received secretly and kept secret. But if one manifests them to a confessor or to some other spiritual person who understands his deceits and malicious designs, the evil one is very much vexed. For he knows that he cannot succeed in his evil undertaking once his deceits have been revealed.[22]

So how does Wimber approach the subject of checks and balances in the process of discernment? He offers some suggestions in his book *Power Healing* where he describes a model in which discerning prayer for healing can take place. One is that such prayer should take place within the context of a corporate, supportive, loving fellowship. He warned against taking on the sole responsibility of praying with someone else alone as he was aware of the dangers of individualism and those who wanted to pray for others for unhealthy reasons. He goes on to give a list of what to expect in the discernment process:

> Inspirations—floods of thoughts, with specific facts, describing situations; dreams and visions, impressions—a deep knowing in one's spirit; Scripture verses—passages that trigger insight for a particular situation; and pains in the body—pains or sensations that correspond to the illness in the person being prayed for.[23]

The difference between Wimber and Ignatius on this point is that Ignatius was concerned to enable a person to discern what God was doing in them. For Wimber the emphasis in discernment was about learning to detect what God was doing in others. So how did he guard against the possibility of self-delusion, or of going off into nebulous mysticism? Like Ignatius, Wimber had a concern that discernment must be placed along the plumb line of Scripture. 'What does the Bible say?' would be a typical response in Vineyard circles. Yet alongside this there was also a concern in Wimber's approach to be open to whatever the Holy Spirit was doing. This was due to a desire not to quench the work of the Spirit and to be open to 'surprise.'

---

22 *Spiritual Exercises*, paragraph 326.
23 *Power Healing*, p 204.

5
Spiritual Warfare

Wimber's call to spiritual warfare, based on his understanding of the coming of the kingdom, has some strong resonances with the work of Ignatius. Ignatius lived at a time when warfare was perhaps more commonplace than today and the mode of operating was hand-to-hand fighting. It is not surprising that he uses some of this imagery in his writings, drawing perhaps upon his own military experiences. This is particularly evident in the beginning of the second 'week' of his *Exercises* with his 'Call of the King.'

The person using the *Exercises,* the exercitant, is invited to imagine a scene where there are towns, villages and people, and into this scene an earthly ruler steps. It is someone with great charisma who commands total respect. This person issues a call, a summons, to anyone who wants to join him in ridding the world of disease, poverty and ignorance. The person doing the exercises is asked to consider how he or she would respond to such a call. The second stage is to imagine that this ruler is Christ himself who issues the same kind of call and the invitation is given to us to respond using the following words:

> Eternal Father…I want and desire and it is my deliberate determination, if only it be thy greater service and praise, to imitate thee in bearing all injuries and abuse and all poverty of spirit and actual poverty too if thy holy majesty wants to choose and receive me to such life and state.[24]

This is not a prayer for the faint-hearted! It comes at the beginning of the second stage of the exercises immediately prior to the start of contemplation on the nativity story. Ignatius' aim was that in meditating upon the life of Christ one must always remember that his call to join him is made to us each day of our lives.

There is remarkable similarity here with the words of Wimber. Whilst there was always an emphasis on intimacy with Christ in worship in Wimber's meetings, his main concern was a call to arms. He likened this age to the time of the occupation of France by the Germans during the Second World War. It was as if the devil had invaded land that rightfully belonged to God, and had taken over. Our task as Christians is to be the resistance movement, to take back the land and to learn to fight a spiritual warfare. Wimber's desire was to 'equip the saints' to do the job that Christ had called them to do. He was concerned to show that the church has been emasculated by failing to recognize that power and authority have already been given to do the works of Jesus here and now. Perhaps his whole mission is encapsulated in these words from his book, *Power Evangelism:*

---

24 *Spiritual Exercises,* paragraph 98.

To a great extent we have practised a cosmetic Christianity because we have misunderstood our initial call to Christ...Our mission is to rescue those who have been taken captive as a result of Adam's fall.[25]

Such a desire to enable ordinary men and women to engage in 'signs and wonders' ministry is one key feature of the appeal of the Vineyard movement. There is no sense here of a hierarchy based on status. Ministry does not reside solely with the professionals on the platform. The last thing Wimber wanted was to inaugurate yet another charismatic cult following. He wanted everyone to engage in warfare, even if this meant losing a few battles on the way and making a few mistakes. The task of evangelism and healing was too massive and too urgent to be left in the hands of just the privileged few.

Both men issued the challenge to follow the call of Christ in redeeming the world. For Ignatius the confidence to do this came from learning to recognize that the Holy Spirit is constantly at work in us, taking us through times of consolation and desolation but always with the knowledge that we are merely sharing in what God is already doing. The starting point for Ignatius was the incarnation. This is where God is seen 'touching' earth. We are invited to share in the life and passion of Christ, to follow the call of the King. For Wimber the confidence to undertake spiritual warfare came from knowing that we have been given the 'tools to do the job.' Although this sounds a very functionalist approach to spirituality, Wimber was merely saying that all the resources of heaven are at our disposal. If we are to follow in the footsteps of Christ then we need to engage with the world in the same way that Christ did in the gospel accounts. Our task is simply to recognize that and to cooperate with the Holy Spirit. In this respect at least, both men are saying the same thing.

25   *Power Evangelism*, pp 25 and 27.

6
Points of Difference

Although there are many points of contact between Ignatian and Vineyard spirituality there are some important differences in theology. It is these differences that have produced significantly divergent outcomes in the way that spirituality is expressed. The resurgent interest in Ignatian spirituality in recent years has been a quiet, unseen affair. It has remained the province of private individual growth in maturity. Wimber's legacy is more visible, perhaps more strident, and although there is within the Vineyard movement a constant desire to be open to change and to engage with contemporary culture, many of the original hallmarks of Wimber's thinking remain.

Creation

Perhaps the most striking difference is the way in which the created order is viewed. How did Ignatius and Wimber perceive the world that God has made?

At the outset of the *Spiritual Exercises* Ignatius touches on the place of 'nature' within the growth of spiritual maturity in what he termed the 'First Principle and Foundation.' This set out the framework within which the remainder of his exercises were to be understood. Ignatius stated that everything on the face of the earth was given to enable us to praise God and that we are to use whatever means we can to do this. Part of this process was to recognize that God can work through all things, therefore we are not to:

> …want health rather than sickness, riches rather than poverty, honour rather than dishonour, long rather than short life and so in all the rest; desiring and choosing only what is most conducive for the end for which we were created.

This insistence that God can be found 'in all things' suffuses the entirety of the *Exercises*. Ignatius picks up this theme again explicitly towards the end of the *Exercises* where he introduces the 'Contemplation on the Love of God.' The person who is doing the exercises is urged to do the following:

> Look how God dwells in creatures, in the elements, giving them being, in the plants vegetating, in the animals feeding them, in men giving them to understand: and so in me giving me being, animating me, giving me sensation and making me understand.[26]

Ignatius suggests that our response to such a meditation on all of God's gifts to us is encapsulated in the words of his famous prayer, *Take and Receive*:

---

26 *Spiritual Exercises*, paragraph 235.

Take Lord, and receive my liberty, my memory, my understanding, and my entire will—all that I have and call my own. You have given it all to me. To you Lord I return it. Everything is yours to do what you will. Give me only your love and your grace. That is enough for me.[27]

The consequence of viewing nature as the place where God's goodness can be seen is profound. In discerning the hand of God, Ignatius was determined to find God in all things—in the gesture of a friend, in a mountain stream and in the beauty of a flower. There was nowhere that God could not be found.

God works and labours for me in all things created upon the face of the earth—that is behaves like one who labours—as in the heavens, elements, plants, fruits, cattle etc giving them being and preserving them.[28]

With such exhortations to discover God, the whole of life becomes a prayer.

Wimber does not display such an emphasis on the created order in his writings. Some have criticized his apparently dualistic view of nature. Nigel Wright, for example, detects in Wimber very sharp distinctions between good and evil, God and the devil, spirit versus body, redemption versus creation.[29] He points out that when the complexities and ambiguities of human existence are reduced to this simplistic structure then none of us are best served. Within such a framework, claims Wright, nature is seen simply as the venue for the spiritual battle. It no longer is a place where God's astonishing creativity and love can be seen.

This may be too stark a criticism of Wimber. He never set out to write a systematic theology and his concern was always with the immediate and urgent task at hand. This meant that some of his theological views changed and evolved in the midst of a busy and demanding schedule. However, the Vineyard movement has struggled at times to make sense of suffering and sickness that is not healed. In his book, *Power Evangelism* he writes that Jesus 'saw an integral unity between sickness and Satan.'[30] Although Wimber qualified this statement by saying that sometimes people are 'just sick' without a spiritual root, the tendency remains for sickness to be placed in the same category as the devil—namely something to be cast out in the context of our on-going spiritual warfare. This then begs the question, can God be discerned in the midst of cancer? Is sickness always a spiritual issue? These are questions that do not easily go away because they are part of the warp and weft of ordinary life. Wimber was aware of this but his paradigm of healing did not offer much solace. At times he acknowledges that God does heal selectively and slowly over a period of time but, on other occasions he writes:

27 *Spiritual Exercises*, paragraph 234.
28 *Spiritual Exercises*, paragraph 236.
29 Nigel Wright, *Charismatic Renewal* (London: SPCK, 1995) p 75.
30 *Power Evangelism*, p 103.

There is another reason—I believe the most fundamental reason—why more people are not healed when prayed for today. We do not seek God as whole-heartedly as we should.[31]

This kind of response can become a recipe for exhaustion, confusion, frustration and ultimately, when God does not heal despite all attempts at persuading him, rebellion. Set within the context of spiritual warfare, a failure to heal or to become 'victorious' over a particular problem constitutes a setback.

The difference between the two could perhaps be summarized in this way. For Ignatius discernment was about discovering the presence of God in creation. For Wimber it was about discerning the power of God over creation. It is very noticeable that the only gospel story that Ignatius uses in his exercises which involves healing is the account of the raising of Lazarus. Ignatius was more con-cerned with engagement with Christ than with power. Wimber, however, drew much of his inspiration in the early days of the Vineyard movement from the healing stories in the Gospel of Luke. What Wimber observed in the life of Christ was a modelling of the gifts of the Spirit in powerful encounters with those whom he met. It was this that provided Wimber's most enduring paradigm.

Evangelism and Prayer

A further distinction between the two lies in the area of evangelism. The cur-rent resurgence of the *Exercises* has undoubtedly produced a profound deepen-ing of relationship with God for those who have used them. They have enabled ordinary men and women to reflect on the work of the Holy Spirit in their lives and to produce a far greater hunger for an intimate and continual relationship with God. Soon after they were written and used by members of the Society of Jesus they were the single most important catalyst for mission. Anyone who has uttered the prayer in response to the Call of the King or dared to pray the words of *Take and Receive* can not remain the same. Those who pray in this way are offer-ing themselves to God to be used at his disposal anywhere in the world. It is not surprising that the early Jesuits became fearless evangelists, with people like Francis Xavier going to Japan and others travelling to parts of South America.

Today the focus of mission amongst those who use Ignatian spirituality is on incarnating the gospel in society. There is a strong emphasis on engagement with social, political and gender issues which is evidenced by the type of articles writ-ten in the Ignatian journal, *The Way*. By contrast Vineyard spirituality sees the advancement of the kingdom more in terms of building new congregations. The emphasis here is primarily on proclaiming the gospel to an unbelieving world combined with a compassion for the poor.

A neutral observer at an Ignatian retreat and a Vineyard conference would notice very different emphases in the purpose of prayer. Vineyard culture places a high priority on intercession. Ignatius gave greater weight to contemplation.

---

31 *Power Healing,* p 169.

Why is this the case? How is a balance between the two maintained?

The predominance of intercessory prayer in Wimber's thinking stems from his two pillars mentioned earlier. Wimber's call to fight the spiritual battle in cooperation with Christ and to only do what the Father is doing has resulted in an outward looking evangelistic/deliverance focus to the work of the church. If the key task of Christians is to usher the kingdom of God into this present age then it follows that intercession will form a major part of this activity. However, Vineyard intercession is very far from a 'shopping list' mentality. Intercession begins with the initiative of God. The primary task is to ask: what is on the heart of God for this person, this church, this locality? Only when some indication of this has been discerned can the intercessor proceed. Inevitably this may mean that intercession does not follow a linear path as it is often conducted corporately with many individuals contributing their perspective on the burden they believe to be on God's heart at that moment.

Within the structure of the Ignatian exercises, intercession on behalf of others is implicit rather than explicit. The world view of Ignatius, that Christians are called to follow the King and to discern God in all things, should inevitably lead the Christian towards intercession. It would be impossible, argued Ignatius, to live in a society surrounded by need and deprivation and not want to take that to God in prayer. Indeed, the early work of the Jesuits was considered highly subversive precisely because their prayer life took them to the farthest flung places in the world with the gospel. Whilst that may still be true in Jesuit circles today it would not be unfair to say that much of the current use of the *Exercises* tends towards private pietism.

Self-Examination

Within each framework how much weight is given to personal reflection and self-examination? Wimber frequently emphasized the 'pilgrim' nature of the Christian life, that we are constantly needing to learn and mature in our faith. Whilst there is an emphasis in Vineyard circles on learning to help others to grow there is less stress on ways in which the individual can learn to develop a lifestyle of honest critical reflection. The raising of awareness of an individual's need to grow would often take place in a corporate context—as a result of a time of worship or through a particularly powerful sermon. But how does one do this on one's own? What happens when we are not in a large gathering with others to help us? What happens between us and God when we are left alone in the privacy of our own room? It is precisely here that Ignatius comes into his own.

With Ignatius the emphasis is far more on the individual in his or her relationship with God, rather than in corporate gatherings. Ignatius suggested that each day should end with a time of self examination. He termed this exercise the 'examen.' Here the exercitant deliberately sets aside time to review the day, to ask God to reveal where he has been, what he has been doing and where perhaps he has fallen short. Ignatius was rigorous in applying checklists to help in the process of examination. Sometimes, he suggests we may use the Ten Commandments as our plumb line, whereas at other times we may recall the sins of pride, anger, envy, lust, gluttony, avarice and sloth and use them as our yardstick. This is how he writes:

> Method for making the General Examen. The first point is to give thanks to God for the benefits received, the second, to ask grace to know our sins and cast them out, the third to ask account of our soul from the hour that we rose up to the present Examen, hour by hour and first as to thoughts, then to words and then to acts, the fourth to ask pardon of God for the faults and the fifth to purpose amendment with his grace.[32]

To the twenty-first-century mind this may seem a morbid and destructive exercise. Yet all of these activities, Ignatius insisted, are to be conducted in the context of knowing that we are loved and held by Christ who gave himself for us. If we are to be serious in following the Call of the King then we need to be aware of the subtle ways in which we fail and can deceive ourselves. Ignatian theology is therefore designed to produce a self-reflective lifestyle, one that is likely to breed humility and an awareness of one's own shortcomings, together with an abiding sense of God's gifts and graces.

7
So What?

Our examination of two very different approaches to spirituality has revealed significant points of contact, together with some clear differences in both emphasis and theology. So does it matter which one we should choose for ourselves? Is it not simply a matter of personal preference? Is Vineyard spirituality for extroverts and Ignatian for the quieter, more reflective amongst us? I believe that we need to draw from both sources.

The strength of Wimber's approach lies in a corporate sense of task which emanates from an intimate experience of God in worship. Wimber greatly heightened expectations of how God works in the present moment. For many this has been both liberating and exhilarating. Wimber presented a God who took delight in engaging with ordinary people. Here was the immanent God, the God of the parlour rather than the God of the High Court—God as our friend, our lover, our healer. It is this God who sends us out into the word to usher in the kingdom. Vineyard spirituality has successfully married the priority of an open, intimate

---

32 *Spiritual Exercises*, paragraph 43.

relationship with Christ with an energetic activism which seeks to advance the kingdom at every opportunity. It is no wonder that this vision has become so attractive and so empowering for many. For Wimber the church is on the move, always engaged with the work of the Father. It is a spirituality which motivates not with a stick, but from a changed and grateful heart.

Despite the undoubted strengths of Vineyard spirituality, it is perhaps weakest when dealing with failure, ambiguity and frustration. With such a strong emphasis on the corporate, what resources can those within the Vineyard movement draw upon during times of solitude? Where is God to be found in the midst of tragedy—when God does not heal, when newly planted churches do not flourish? Is this world simply to be seen as the venue for spiritual battle? Can God be found in the mundane, the ordinary, the unspectacular, when there are no apparent manifestations of the Spirit at all? Is the advancement of the kingdom of God always visible, observable, measurable? How does Vineyard spirituality maintain itself when nothing appears to be happening? Or to put the question in Ignatian terms, does Vineyard spirituality have a theology of 'desolation'?

It is in answer to these questions that Ignatian spirituality offers a structure within which prayer can continue and God can be found. Whilst Ignatius shared Wimber's call to arms to do the work of Christ, he was aware that God could be discovered everywhere. There were no preconditions by which the activity of the Spirit should be measured. According to Ignatius our task is to develop the spiritual antennae to discern his presence and the *Exercises* provide a range of ways of learning how to do just this. The great strength of his *Exercises* are that they are firmly rooted in the Scriptures with their focus on the person and work of Christ.

The weakness of Ignatian spirituality today lies not so much in the *Exercises* themselves, but in the way in which they can be used. Ignatian spirituality can become a very interior, private affair where God's dealings with the soul become so profound and deep as to be unutterable to anyone else save a spiritual director. But making the *Exercises* a purely individual affair, divorced from the life of the church, was far from the intention of Ignatius. If this happens then using the *Exercises* becomes a form of spiritual narcissism.[33] The intention of Ignatius was to prepare people for apostolic ministry, not to encourage navel gazing. In contemporary postmodern culture there is a quest for private forms of spirituality. It would be a tragedy if the *Exercises* were hijacked for this purpose alone.

This is why the two spiritualities can benefit from each other. The Vineyard values of intimacy with Christ and eager expectancy combined with the reflective, challenging structure for prayer offered by Ignatius is surely a marriage worth considering. I wonder if Ignatius and Wimber are chatting at this moment over a cup of celestial filter coffee, wishing that their followers could at least begin by shaking hands.

---

33 See 'Forgotten Truths' by Gerard Hughes in *The Way of Ignatius Loyola* edited by Philip Sheldrake (London: SPCK, 1991).